Anthology of R & B SONGS

PIANO • VOCAL • GUITAR

G000298752

ISBN 978-1-4234-9441-6

HAL•LEONARD®
CORPORATION

7777 W. BLUEMOUND RD. P.O. Box

9140000025920

Visit Hal Leonard Online at
www.halleonard.com

ABC

Words and Music by ALPHONSO MIZELL,
FREDERICK PERREN, DEKE RICHARDS and BERRY GORDY

AIN'T NO MOUNTAIN HIGH ENOUGH

Words and Music by NICKOLAS ASHFORD
and VALERIE SIMPSON

Now, if you need me, call ___ me. No mat-ter where you
I set you free? _____ I told you you could

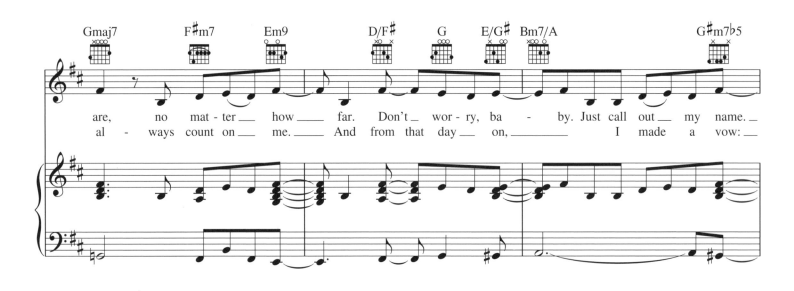

are, no mat-ter ___ how ___ far. Don't ___ wor-ry, ba - by. Just call out ___ my name. ___
al - ways count on ___ me. ___ And from that day ___ on, _____ I made a vow: ___

___ I'll be there in a hur - ry. ___ You don't have to wor - ry, 'cause, ba - by, there
___ I'll be there when you want ___ me, ___ some way ___ some - how. ___ 'Cause, ba - by, there

AIN'T NO SUNSHINE

Words and Music by
BILL WITHERS

BALL OF CONFUSION
(That's What the World Is Today)

Words and Music by NORMAN WHITFIELD
and BARRETT STRONG

Moderately slow

Peo-ple mov-in' out, peo-ple mov-in' in, why?___ Be-cause of the col-or of their skin,

run, run, run___ but you sho' can't hide.___ An

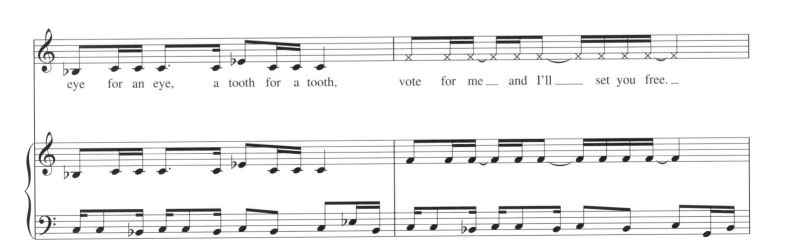

eye for an eye, a tooth for a tooth, vote for me___ and I'll___ set you free.___

ball of con-fu - sion, __ oh __ yeah, __ that's what the world is to-day.

The sale of pills __ is at an all - time high,

young folks walk-in' 'round __ with their heads in the sky, __ cit-ies a - flame __ in the sum-mer-time, __ and, oh, __

_____ the beat goes on. __

Fear in the air, ten-sion ev-'ry-where, __ un-em-ploy-ment ris-ing fast, the Bea-tle's new rec-ord's a gas

and the on - ly safe place __ to live is on an In - di-an res-er-va-tion and the band played

on.

Eve of de-struc - tion, tax de - duc - tion, cit - y in-spec-tors, bill col-lec-tors,

AIN'T TOO PROUD TO BEG

Words and Music by EDWARD HOLLAND
and NORMAN WHITFIELD

Moderately fast

I know you wan-na leave me, but I re-fuse to let you go.

If I have to beg, plead for your sym-pa-thy, I don't mind

'cause you mean that much to me. Ain't too proud to beg, and you know it.
(Ooh, sweet dar -

ALL IN LOVE IS FAIR

Words and Music by
STEVIE WONDER

Recorded a half step lower.

BABY WORKOUT

Words and Music by JACKIE WILSON
and ALONZO TUCKER

BETWEEN THE SHEETS

Words and Music by O'KELLY ISLEY,
RONALD ISLEY, RUDOLPH ISLEY, ERNIE ISLEY,
MARVIN ISLEY and CHRIS JASPER

Moderately slow Funk

1. Hey, girl, __ ain't __ no mys -
2. Ooh, girl, __ let __ me hold __
3.,4. *(See additional lyrics)*

- ter - y, at __ least __ as far as I __ can see. I wan-na keep __ you here __
__ you tight, and you know __ I'll make you feel __ al-right. Oh, ba - by girl, just cling __

40

Additional Lyrics

3. Ooh, girl, I'll love you all night long.
   And I know you felt it comin' on.
   Ooh, darling, just taste my love.
   Oh, you taste so sweet,
   Sharing our love between the sheets.

4. Hey, girl, what's your fantasy?
   I'll take you there to that ecstasy.
   Oh, girl, you blow my mind;
   I'll always be your freak.
   Let's make sweet love between the sheets.

BRICK HOUSE

Words and Music by LIONEL RICHIE, RONALD LaPREAD,
WALTER ORANGE, MILAN WILLIAMS,
THOMAS McCLARY and WILLIAM KING

CALL ME
(Come Back Home)

Words and Music by WILLIE MITCHELL,
AL GREEN and AL JACKSON, JR.

ly. _____ Yeah. _____ Go on and take your time _____

'cause you're on - ly los - in' me.

Hey, ___ love ___ is a long ___ ways ___ from here; ___

___ tell you, it's all ___ in the way ___ you ___ feel. ___

CAN'T GET ENOUGH OF YOUR LOVE, BABE

Words and Music by
BARRY WHITE

CLOUD NINE

Words and Music by BARRETT STRONG
and NORMAN WHITFIELD

Moderately, with double-time feeling

Child - hood part of my life, it was-n't ver - y pret - ty. You see, I was

born and raised _____ in the slums of the cit - y, it was a

one room shack that slept ten oth - er chil - dren be - sides me. _____ We

COLD SWEAT, PT. 1

Words and Music by JAMES BROWN
and ALFRED JAMES ELLIS

COOL JERK

Words and Music by
DONALD STORBALL

to speak. ___
they speak. ___

On their fac - es they wear a sil - ly smirk 'cause they know ___
On their fac - es they don't ___ wear a smirk 'cause they know ___

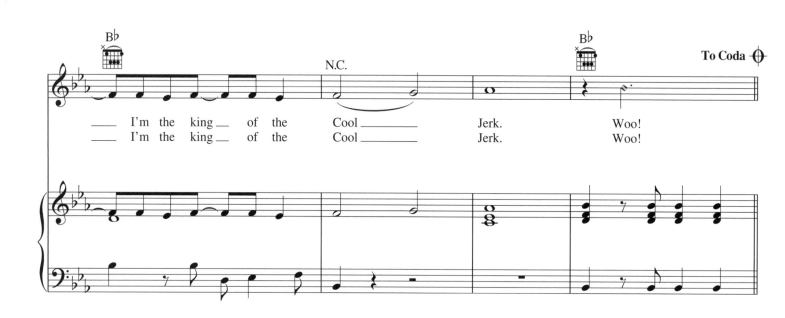

___ I'm the king ___ of the Cool _____ Jerk. Woo!
___ I'm the king ___ of the Cool _____ Jerk. Woo!

To Coda

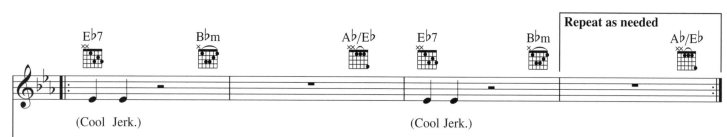

Repeat as needed

(Cool Jerk.) (Cool Jerk.)

Ha. Look at those guys looking at me like I'm the fool. But deep down inside they know I'm cool.
But now the moment of truth has finally come when I'm gonna show you some of that Cool Jerk.
Now give me a little bass with those Eighty-eights. Ah, you're cooking, uh, you're smoking.
Now I want-a hear everybody. Ah....

CRUISIN'

Words and Music by WILLIAM "SMOKEY" ROBINSON
and MARVIN TARPLIN

Moderately slow

Ba - by, let's cruise a - way from
Ba - by, to - night be - longs to
Ba - by, let's cruise, let's float, let's

here. us. glide.

Don't be con - fused, the way is
Ev - 'ry - thing's right, do what you
Let's o - pen love and go in -

DEDICATED TO THE ONE I LOVE

Words and Music by LOWMAN PAULING
and RALPH BASS

D.S. al Coda I

DO RIGHT WOMAN DO RIGHT MAN

Words and Music by DAN PENN
and CHIPS MOMAN

Take me to heart _____ and

I'll al - ways love you,

and no - bod - y _____ can

EVERYBODY NEEDS SOMEBODY TO LOVE

Words and Music by BERT BERNS,
SOLOMAN BURKE and GERRY WEXLER

FOR YOUR PRECIOUS LOVE

By ARTHUR BROOKS, RICHARD BROOKS
and JERRY BUTLER

Lyrics:

Your pre-cious love _____ means more to me ____ than an-y love could ev-er be. _____ For when I want-ed you, _____ I was so lone-ly ___ and so _ blue,

GET READY

Words and Music by
WILLIAM "SMOKEY" ROBINSON

I

nev - er met a girl who makes ___ me feel ___ the way that
wan - na play ___ hide and seek ___ with love, ___ let me re -
All ___ my ___ friends should - n't want me to, ___ I un - der -

you do. (It's al - right.) ___ Wh en - ev - er I'm asked ___ who makes
mind you. (It's al - right.) ___ The lov - ing you're gon - na miss,
stand it. (Be al - right.) ___ I hope ___ I'll get ___ to you be -

GIMME SOME LOVIN'

Words and Music by STEVE WINWOOD,
MUFF WINWOOD and SPENCER DAVIS

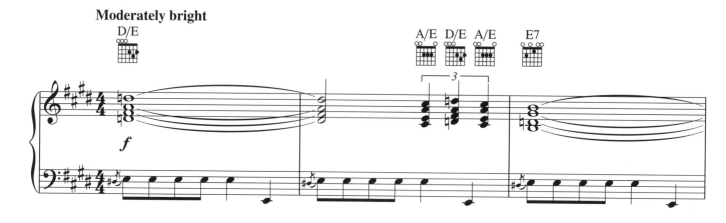

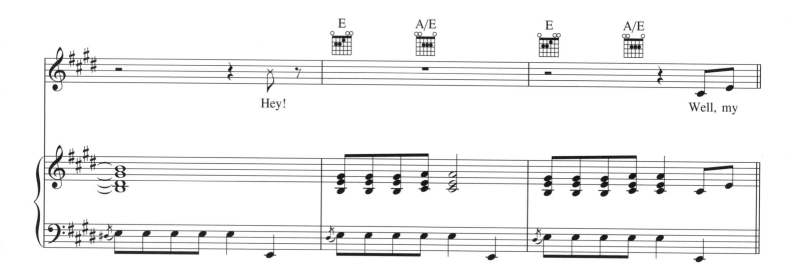

Hey!

Well, my

tem - p'ra - ture's   ris - ing   and   my   feet   on   the   floor.
feel   so   good; ___   ev - 'ry - thing   is   sound - ing   hot.
feel   so   good; ___   ev - 'ry - bod - y's   get - tin'   high.

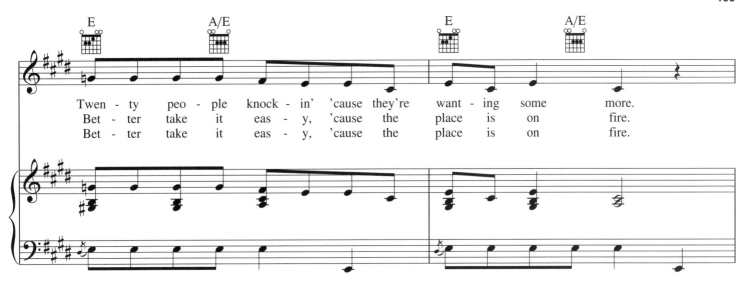

Twen - ty peo - ple knock - in' 'cause they're want - ing some more.
Bet - ter take it eas - y, 'cause the place is on fire.
Bet - ter take it eas - y, 'cause the place is on fire.

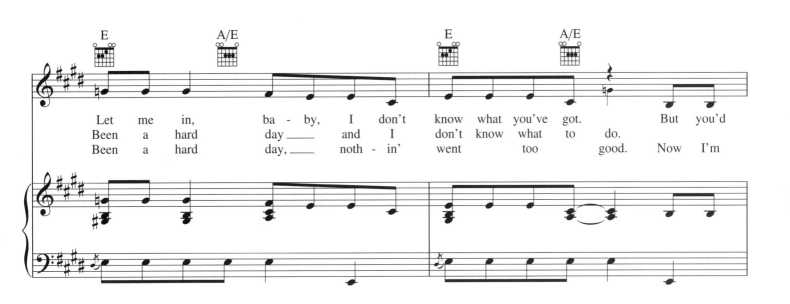

Let me in, ba - by, I don't know what you've got. But you'd
Been a hard day____ and I don't know what to do.
Been a hard day,____ noth - in' went too good. Now I'm

bet - ter take it eas - y. This _____ place is hot.
Wait a min - ute, ba - by. It could hap - pen to you.
gon - na re - lax, hon - ey. Ev - 'ry - bod - y should. __

GIVE IT UP OR TURNIT A LOOSE

Words and Music by
CHARLES FRED BOBBITT

Slowly, with a double-time feeling

al - right, _____ hold - ing
with all my might, _ hold ya

on _ ain't no use. _
tight _ 'cause I love ya so. _

2nd time D.C. and Fade

HARD TO HANDLE

Words and Music by ALLEN JONES,
ALVERTIS BELL and OTIS REDDING

1.,3. Ba - by, here I am, I'm a man on the scene.
2. Ac - tions speak loud-er than words, and I'm a man of great ex - per - ience.
4. *Instrumental*

I can give you what you want but you got to come home with me.
I know you got an - oth - er man, but I can love you bet-ter than him.

I got some good old lov - in' and I've got some more in store.
Take my hand, don't be a - fraid. I want to prove ev - 'ry word I say.

Vocal ad lib. to end

GROOVE ME

Words and Music by
KING FLOYD

Uh! __ Oh, __ sook-y, sook-y now. Hey! Ow, uh,

come on, ba - by. Hey __ there, sug - ar dar - ling, __
Hey there, sug - ar dar - ling, __

let me tell you some - thing, _ girl, __ I've been try - ing to say, __ now.
come on, give me some - thing, _ girl, __ I've been need - ing for days. __

Recorded a half step lower.

HEATWAVE
(Love Is Like a Heatwave)

Words and Music by EDWARD HOLLAND,
LAMONT DOZIER and BRIAN HOLLAND

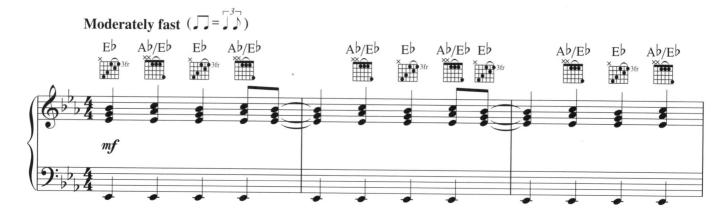

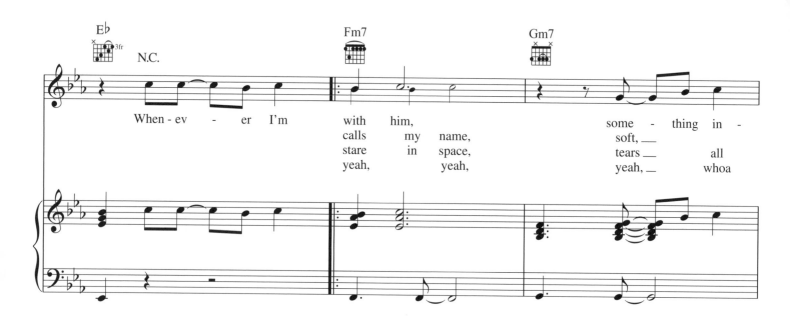

When-ev-er I'm with him, calls my name, some-thing in-
stare in space, soft, tears all
yeah, yeah, yeah, all whoa

side low, sweet and plain, starts to burn-in' I feel, yeah,
o-ver my face. I can't ex-plain it, don't un-der-
ho. Yeah, yeah, yeah,

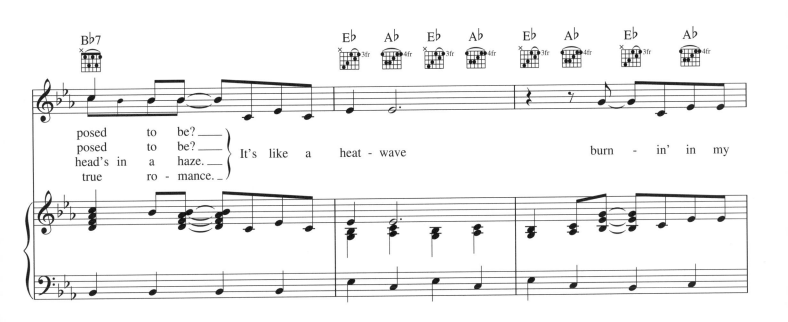

HOW SWEET IT IS
(To Be Loved by You)

Words and Music by EDWARD HOLLAND,
LAMONT DOZIER and BRIAN HOLLAND

HOLD ON I'M COMIN'

Words and Music by ISAAC HAYES
and DAVID PORTER

I CAN'T STAND THE RAIN

Words and Music by DON BRYANT,
ANN PEEBLES and BERNARD MILLER

I can't stand the rain 'gainst my

win - dow, __ ho, __ bring-in' back sweet mem-o-ries. __ I can't stand the

rain a-gainst my __ win - dow, __ ho, __ be-cause he's not here with
rain a-gainst my __ win - dow, __ ho, __ bring-in' back sweet mem - o -
rain a-gainst my __ win - dow, __ ho, __ bring-in' back sweet mem - o -

8vb throughout

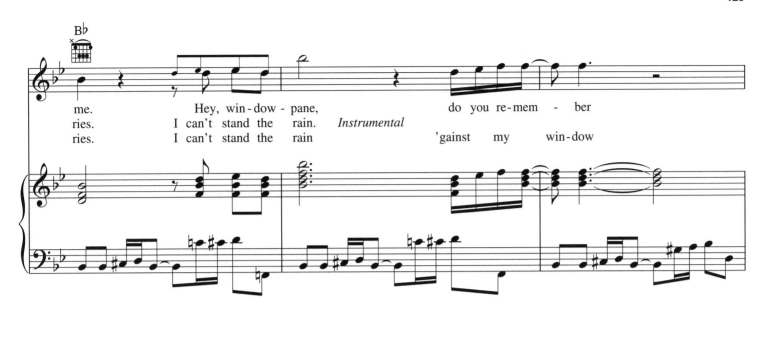

me.　　　　Hey, win-dow-pane,　　　　do you re-mem - ber
ries.　　I can't stand the rain. *Instrumental*
ries.　　I can't stand the rain　　'gainst my win-dow

how sweet it　used to be? ___
　　　　　Instrumental ends ⎫
'cause he's not　here with me. ___⎭

When we were to-
Whoa,　emp - ty

geth - er,　huh, ___ huh,　　　　ev - 'ry-thing　was so　grand. ___　Yes, it was.
pil - low,　huh, ___ huh,　　　　where his head　used to lay,　　yeah.

I FORGOT TO BE YOUR LOVER

Words and Music by WILLIAM BELL
and BOOKER T. JONES, JR.

I GOT A WOMAN

Words and Music by RAY CHARLES
and RENALD J. RICHARD

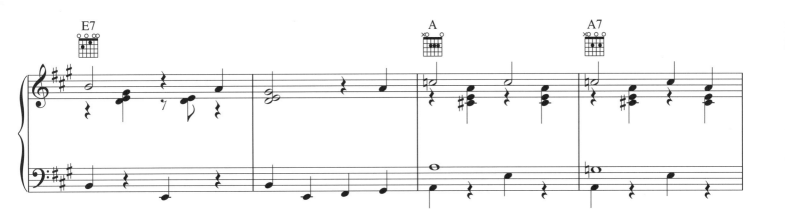

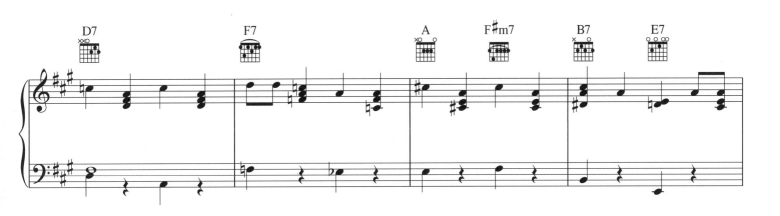

I JUST WANT TO CELEBRATE

Words and Music by NICK ZESSES
and DINO FEKARIS

I SAY A LITTLE PRAYER

Lyric by HAL DAVID
Music by BURT BACHARACH

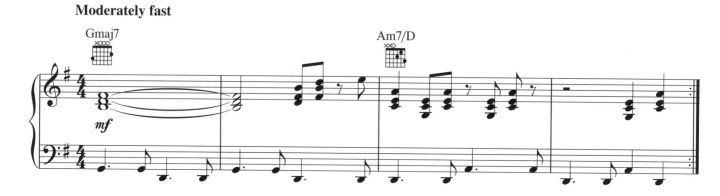

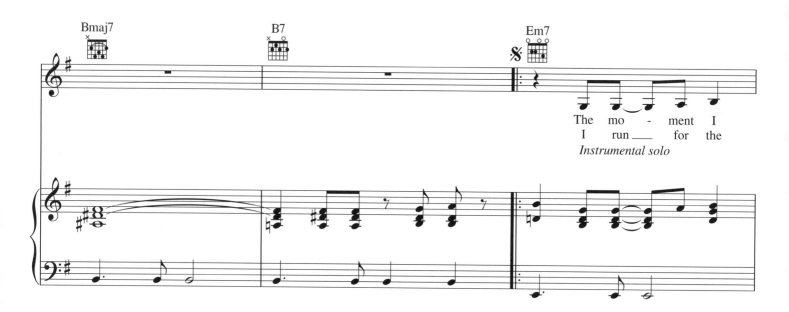

The mo - ment I
I run ___ for the
Instrumental solo

wake up,   be - fore ___ I put   on my   make - up,   I
bus, dear.   While rid - ing, I think of   us, dear.   I
(I

I'LL BE THE OTHER WOMAN

Words and Music by HOMER BANKS
and CARL HAMPTON

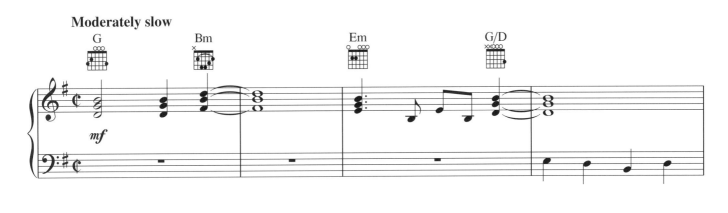

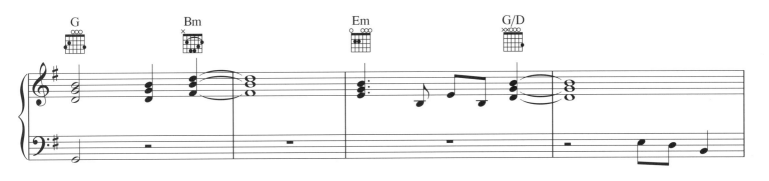

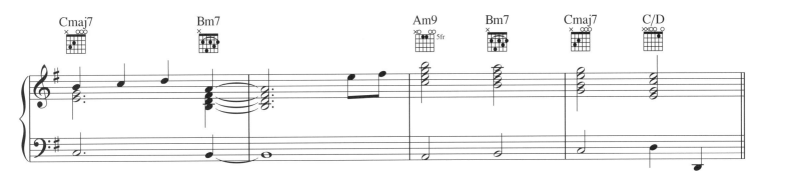

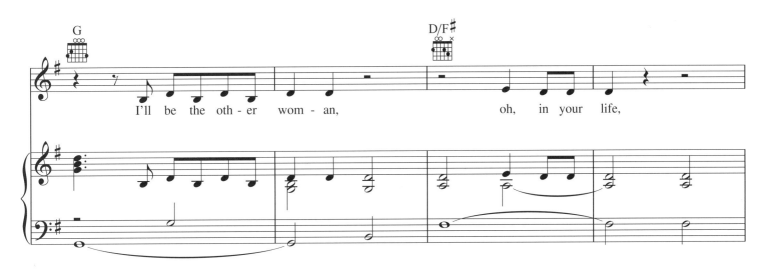

I'll be the oth-er wom-an,   oh, in your life,

I THANK YOU

Words and Music by ISAAC HAYES
and DAVID PORTER

You did-n't have to love ___ me like you did, but you did, but you
did-n't have to squeeze, ___ but you did, but you did, but you
did-n't have to shake ___ it, but you did, but you did, but you

did, and I thank you. You did-n't have to love ___ me like you
did, and I thank you. You did-n't have to hold ___ me, but you
did, and I thank you. You did-n't have to make ___ it like you

I WANT YOU BACK

Words and Music by FREDDIE PERREN,
ALPHONSO MIZELL, BERRY GORDY and DEKE RICHARDS

I'M GONNA TEAR YOUR PLAYHOUSE DOWN

Words and Music by
EARL RANDLE

I'm gon-na tear your play-house down ___ room ___ by room. ___

I'M GONNA MAKE YOU LOVE ME

Words and Music by LEON HUFF,
KENNETH GAMBLE and JERRY ROSS

I'm gon-na do all the things for you a man___ wants a girl to do,
My love is strong-er, see, I know you'll nev-er get tired___ of me,

oh, ba-by.___
oh, ba-by.___

I'll sac-ri-fice for you, I'll
I'm gon-na use ev-'ry trick in the book to

e-ven do___ wrong,___ too,
try my best to get you hooked,

oh, ba-by.___
oh, ba-by.___

Ev-'ry
Ev-'ry

2nd time D.S. and Fade

I'VE BEEN LOVING YOU TOO LONG

Words and Music by OTIS REDDING
and JERRY BUTLER

1. I've been lov-ing you _____
2. (See additional lyrics)

too long _____ to stop now. _____

You are tired _____ and you

Additional Lyrics

2. With you, my life has been so wonderful;
I can't stop now.
You are tired,
And your love is growing cold;
My love is growing stronger,
As our affair grows old.
I've been loving you, a little too long;
I don't wanna stop now.

IF LOVING YOU IS WRONG I DON'T WANT TO BE RIGHT

Words and Music by HOMER BANKS,
CARL HAMPTON and RAYMOND JACKSON

If lov-in' you is wrong, I don't want to be right. If

Am I wrong to fall so deep-ly in love with you,

be-ing right means be-ing with-out you, I'd rath-er live a wrong-do-ing life. Your

know-ing I got a wife and two lit-tle chil-dren de-pend-ing on me, too? But

IF I WERE YOUR WOMAN

Words and Music by CLAY McMURRAY,
PAMELA SAWYER and GLORIA JONES

Moderate Ballad, with a beat

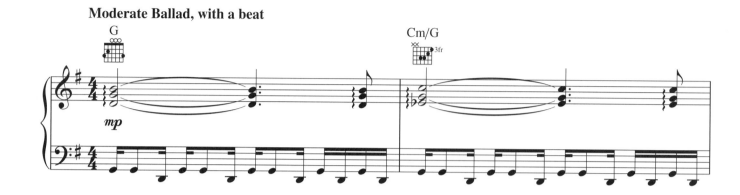

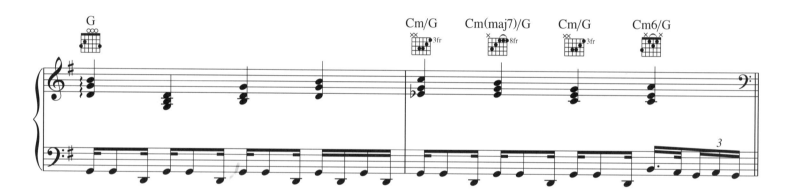

If I were your wom - an ____ and you were my man,

D.S. al Coda

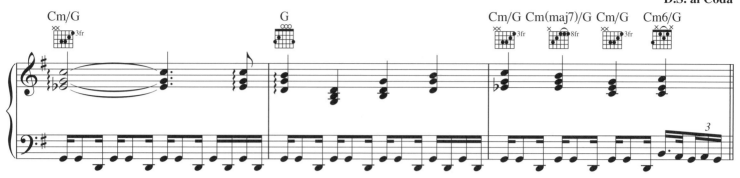

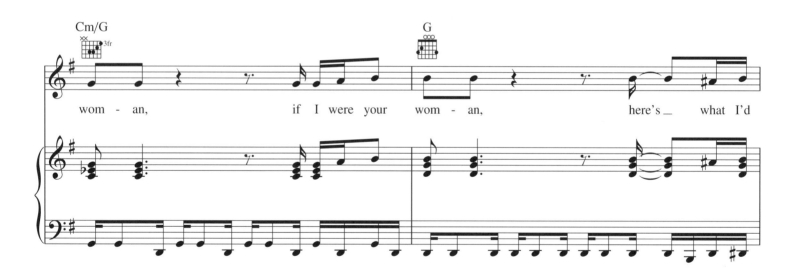

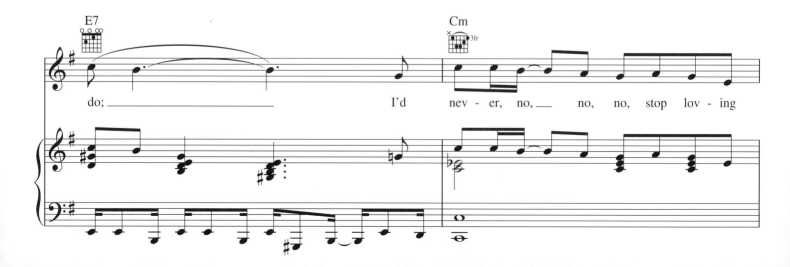

IN THE MIDNIGHT HOUR

Words and Music by STEVE CROPPER
and WILSON PICKETT

IT TAKES TWO

Words and Music by WILLIAM STEVENSON
and SYLVIA MOY

1. One can have a dream, ba-by; two can make that dream so
2.,3. (See additional lyrics)

real. One can talk a-bout be-ing in love; two can

say how it real-ly feels. One can wish up-on

Additional Lyrics

2. One can have a broken heart, living in misery;
   Two can really ease the pain like the perfect remedy.
   One can be alone in a crowd; like an island, he's all alone.
   Two can make it just-a any place seem just like being home.
   Chorus

3. One can go out to a movie, looking for a special treat;
   Two can make that a single movie something really kind-a sweet.
   One can take a walk in the moonlight, thinking that it's really nice;
   Ah, but two walking a-hand in hand is like adding just a pinch of spice.
   Chorus

IT'S YOUR THING

Words and Music by RUDOLPH ISLEY,
RONALD ISLEY and O'KELLY ISLEY

KNOCK ON WOOD

Words and Music by EDDIE FLOYD
and STEVE CROPPER

Additional Lyrics

3. Ain't no secret that a woman can feel my love come up.
   You got me seeing, she really sees that, that I get enough.
   Just one touch from you, baby, you know it means so much.
   It's like thunder, lightning;
   The way you love me is frightening.
   I think I better knock knock knock knock knock on wood.

LET'S GET IT ON

Words and Music by MARVIN GAYE
and ED TOWNSEND

Slow Soul beat

I've __ been real-ly try - in', ba - by, __ try-in' to hold __ back this feel-

in' for so ___ long. And if you feel __ like __ I feel, __ ba-by,

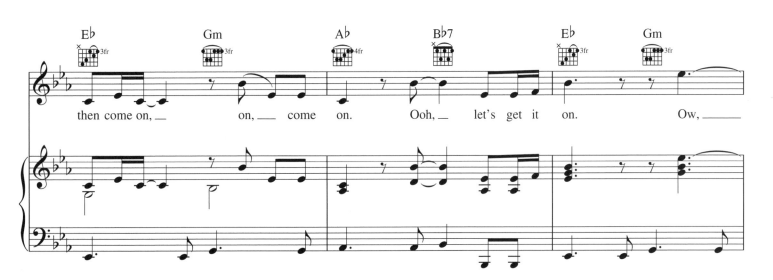

then come on, __ on, __ come on. Ooh, __ let's get it on. Ow, _____

LEAN ON ME

Words and Music by
BILL WITHERS

LET'S GROOVE

Words and Music by MAURICE WHITE
and WAYNE VAUGHN

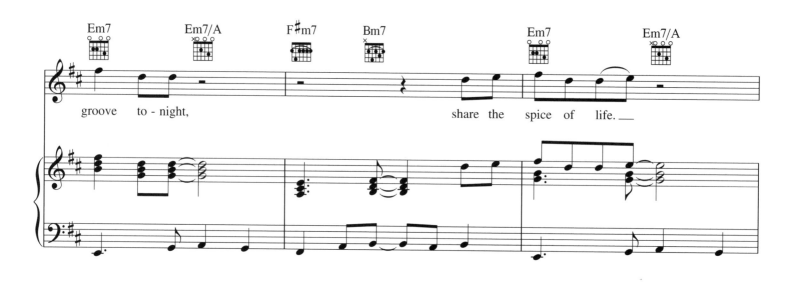

LET'S STAY TOGETHER

Words and Music by AL GREEN,
WILLIE MITCHELL and AL JACKSON, JR.

LICKING STICK - LICKING STICK

Words and Music by JAMES BROWN,
BOBBY BYRD and ALFRED ELLIS

THE LOVE YOU SAVE

Words and Music by BERRY GORDY,
ALPHONSO MIZELL, FREDDIE PERREN
and DEKE RICHARDS

LIVING IN AMERICA
from the Motion Picture ROCKY IV

Words and Music by DAN HARTMAN
and CHARLIE MIDNIGHT

Medium Funk

246

LOVE AND HAPPINESS

Words and Music by AL GREEN
and MABON HODGES

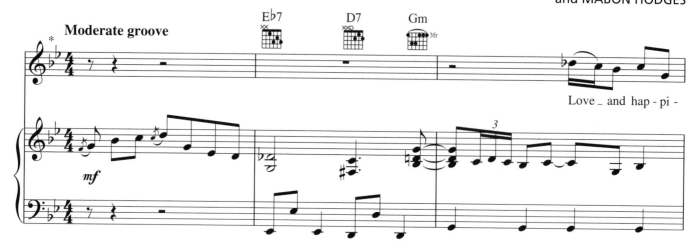

Recorded a half step higher.

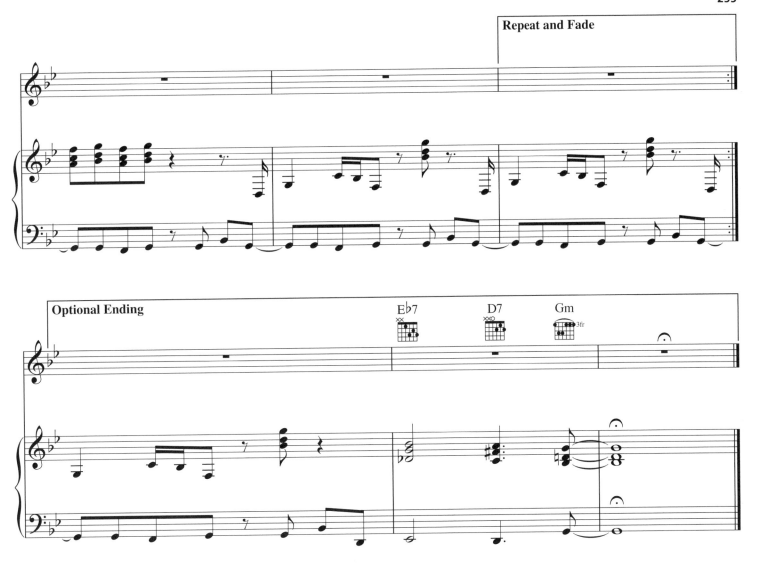

Additional Lyrics

Love is... wait a minute.
Love is...

Walkin' together,
Talkin' together,

Singin' together,
Playin' together.

Playin', wanna moan, say,
Mmm...

Moan for love.
Mmm...

Let me moan for love.
Mmm...

LOVE'S HOLIDAY

Words and Music by MAURICE WHITE
and CLARENCE SCARBOROUGH

Would you mind
Would you mind

if I touched, if I kissed, if I
if I looked in your eyes 'til I'm

LOVELY DAY

Words and Music by SKIP SCARBOROUGH
and BILL WITHERS

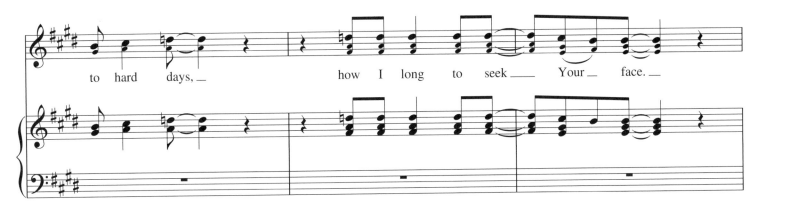

to hard days, ___ how I long to seek ___ Your ___ face. ___

(Ooh.) _____ one look to You and then I
When blue skies turn to grey, ___

know it's gon - na be ___ a, _____ it's gon - na be ___ a love - ly

Moderately slow

E7(no3rd)

day. _____

Then I look _ to You _ and the world is all right with me.

_ and the world _ is all _ right _ with me.
_ right, _ all _ right _ with me.) _

Just one look _ to You _____ and I know _ it's
(Just one look _ to You _ and I know it's gon - na be) _

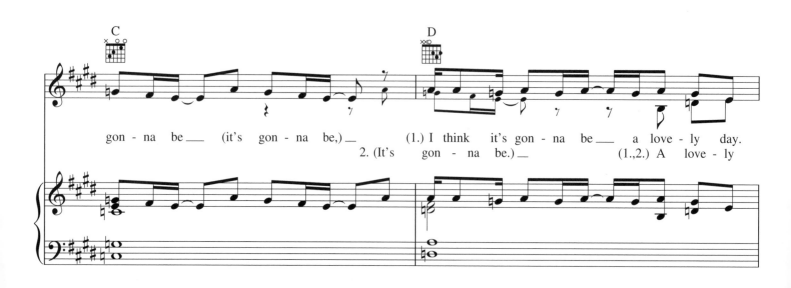

gon - na be _ (it's gon - na be,) _ (1.) I think it's gon - na be _ a love - ly day.
2. (It's gon - na be.) _ (1.,2.) A love - ly

*High vocal harmony part sung first time only.

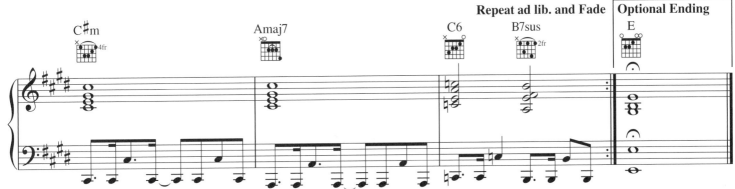

MAMA HE TREATS YOUR DAUGHTER MEAN

Words and Music by JOHNNY WALLACE,
HERB LANCE and CHARLIE SINGLETON

Moderately fast Blues

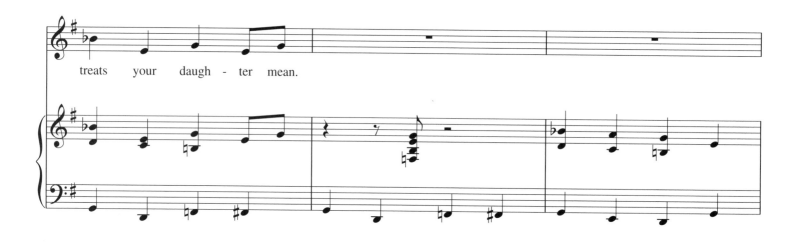

MUSTANG SALLY

Words and Music by
BONNY RICE

F7
Sal - ly,
think you bet - ter
slow your mus - tang down.
C7
G7
You been run - ning all o - ver the town now.
F7
N.C.
Oh! I guess I'll have to put your flat feet on the ground.
C7

All you want to do is ride a-round, Sal-ly. Ride, Sal-ly, ride.____

All you want to do is ride a-round, Sal-ly. Ride, Sal-ly, ride.____

____ All you want to do is ride a-round, Sal-ly.

MESS AROUND

Words and Music by
AHMET ERTEGUN

With a beat

(Optional bass throughout)

Ah, you can talk a-bout the pit bar-be-cue,
ev-'ry-bod-y was juiced, you can bet your soul,
I____ say,____ "Stop," don't you move a peg; when
band's____ gon-na play from nine to one,
see____ that____ girl with the dia-mond ring,

MR. PITIFUL

Words and Music by OTIS REDDING
and STEVE CROPPER

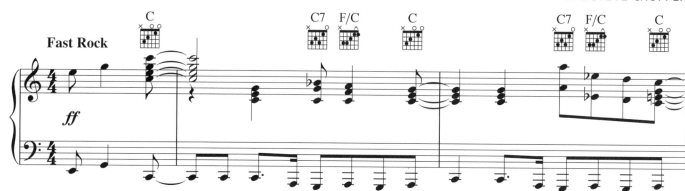

1. They call __ me Mis-ter __ Pit - i - ful;
2. (See additional lyrics)

ba - by, that's my name. __ They call __ me Mis-ter __

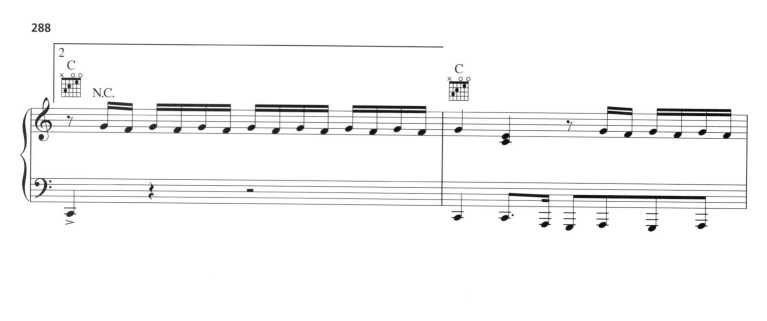

How can I ex - plain to you __

some - bod - y act - ing so ver - y blue?

Additional Lyrics

2. They call me Mr. Pitiful; yes, everybody knows, now.
   They call me Mr. Pitiful most every place I go.
   But nobody seems to understand, now, what makes a man sing such a sad song,
   When he lost everything, when he lost everything he had.

MY GUY

Words and Music by
WILLIAM "SMOKEY" ROBINSON

Moderately

Noth - ing you could say could tear _____ me a - way from my _____
Noth - ing you could do could make _____ me un - true to my _____

_____ guy. _ (My guy.) _ Noth - ing you could do 'cause I'm _____
_____ guy. _ (My guy.) _ Noth - ing you could buy could make _____

_____ stuck like glue to my _____ guy. _ (My guy.) _ I'm
_____ me tell a lie to my _____ guy. _ (My guy.) _ I

NEVER TOO MUCH

Words and Music by
LUTHER VANDROSS

Moderate Funk

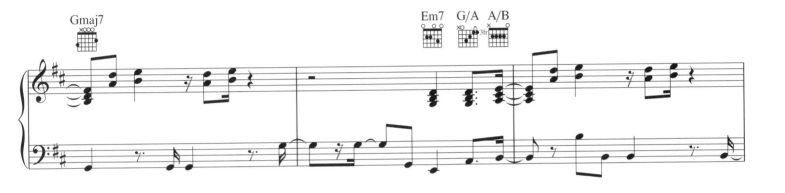

I can't fool my - self.___ I don't want no - bod -
Woke up to - day,___ looked at your pic -

NOWHERE TO RUN

Words and Music by LAMONT DOZIER,
BRIAN HOLLAND and EDWARD HOLLAND

OOO BABY BABY

Words and Music by WILLIAM "SMOKEY" ROBINSON
and WARREN MOORE

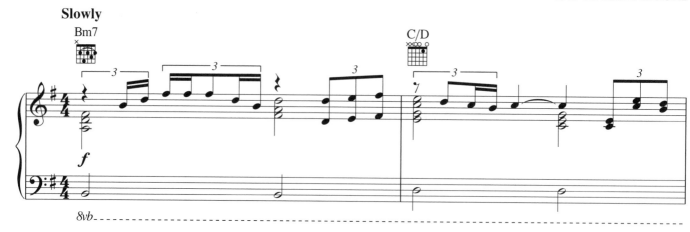

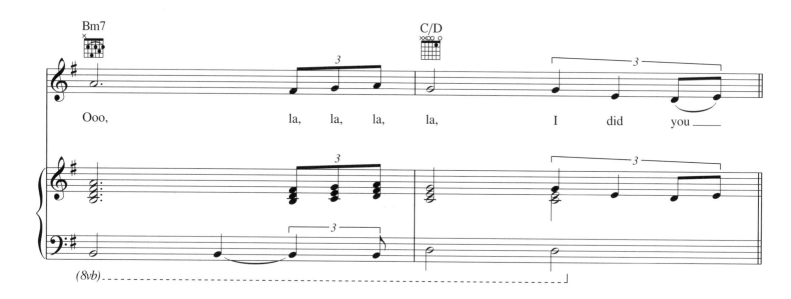

Ooo, la, la, la, la, I did you ___

wrong; ___ my heart ___ went out to play, and in the game, ___ I

takes, ___ I know ___ I've made a few, but I'm on - ly

OVERJOYED

Words and Music by
STEVIE WONDER

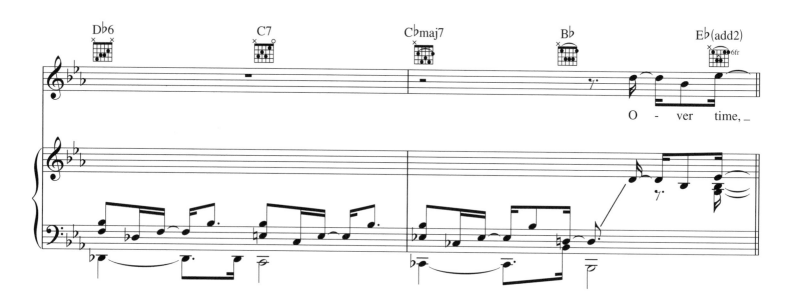

O - ver time,

I've _ been build - ing _ my cas - tle _ of love _
I _ have picked _ out a per - fect _ come true, _
I _ have pain - ful - ly turned _ eve - ry stone _

PAIN IN MY HEART

Words and Music by
NAOMI NEVILLE

Moderate Blues Ballad

Pain in my heart, it's treat-in' me cold.

Where can my ba-by be? Lord, no one know.

Pain in my heart, just won't let me sleep.

PLEASE ACCEPT MY LOVE

Words and Music by B.B. KING
and SAUL BIHARI

till I make you un - der - stand. _____

N.C.

If you on - ly, on - ly knew _____

just how much I _____ love you. _____

PLEASE MR. POSTMAN

Words and Music by ROBERT BATEMAN,
GEORGIA DOBBINS, WILLIAM GARRETT,
FREDDIE GORMAN and BRIAN HOLLAND

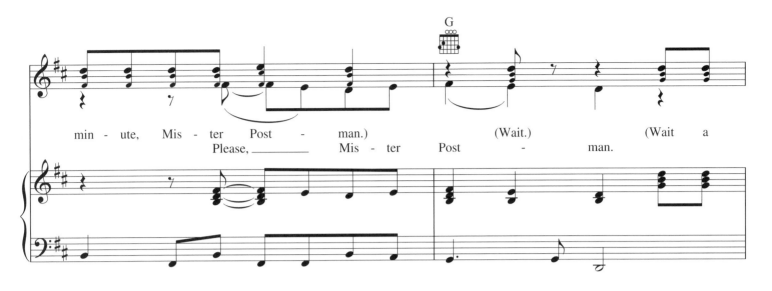

min - ute, Mis - ter Post - man.) (Wait.) (Wait a

Please, _____ Mis - ter Post - man.

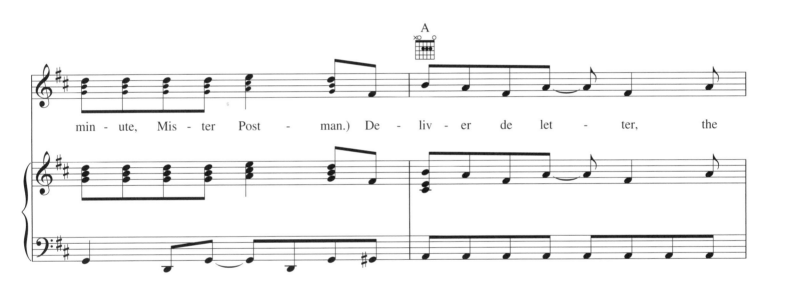

min - ute, Mis - ter Post - man.) De - liv - er de let - ter, the

soon - er de bet - ter.

Optional Ending

Repeat ad lib. and Fade

REACH OUT AND TOUCH
(Somebody's Hand)

Words and Music by NICKOLAS ASHFORD
and VALERIE SIMPSON

REACH OUT, I'LL BE THERE

Words and Music by BRIAN HOLLAND,
LAMONT DOZIER and EDWARD HOLLAND

Moderately

Now if you feel that you can't go on _____ be - cause
lost and a - bout to give up _____ 'cause your
tell the way you hang your head, _____ you're with - out

all of your hope is gone, _____ and your life
best just ain't good e - nough _____ and you feel
love and now you're a - fraid _____ and through your

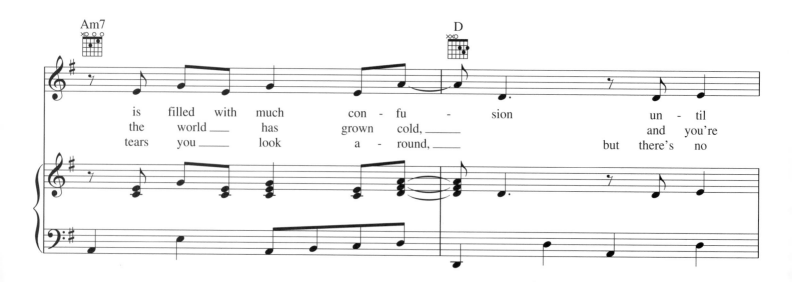

is filled with much con - fu - sion un - til
the world _____ has grown cold, _____ and you're
tears you _____ look a - round, _____ but there's no

RESPECT

Words and Music by
OTIS REDDING

Moderately fast

RESPECT YOURSELF

Words and Music by MACK RICE
and LUTHER INGRAM

RIBBON IN THE SKY

Words and Music by
STEVIE WONDER

Slowly, with expression

Oh, so

THE RIGHT TIME

Words and Music by
LEW HERMAN

Medium Blues tempo

You know the

night-time, dar-lin',   is the right time _____   to be _____
moth-er, now,   hadn't a dime, now. _____   My fa-

(I'm A)
ROAD RUNNER

Words and Music by EDWARD HOLLAND, JR.,
BRIAN HOLLAND and LAMONT DOZIER

Moderately with a driving beat

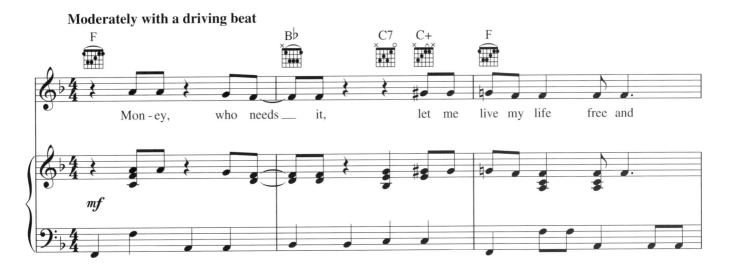

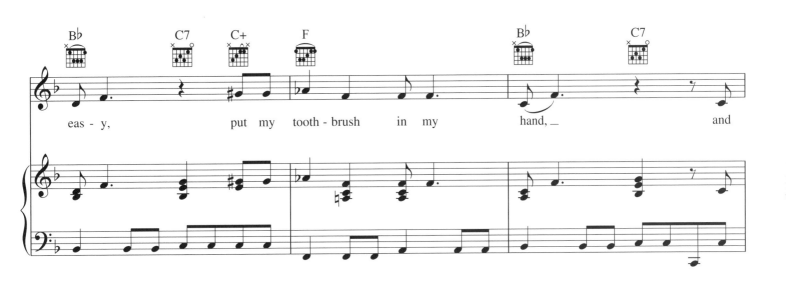

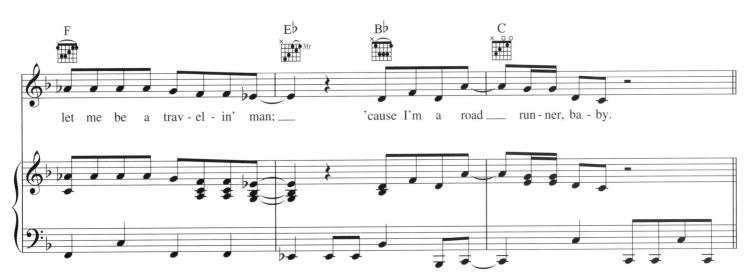

2nd time D.S. and Fade

THE SECRET GARDEN
(Sweet Seduction)

Words and Music by QUINCY JONES,
SIEDAH GARRETT, ROD TEMPERTON
and ELDRA DeBARGE

Slow groove

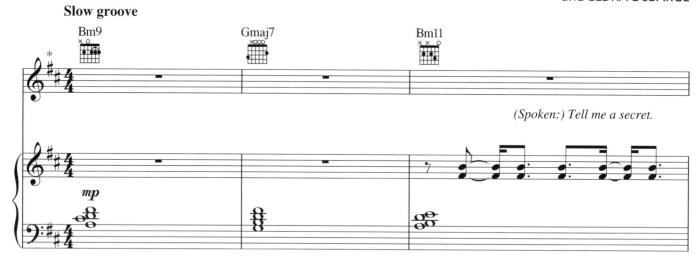

(Spoken:) Tell me a secret.

I don't just want to know about any secret of yours, I want to know about one special secret.

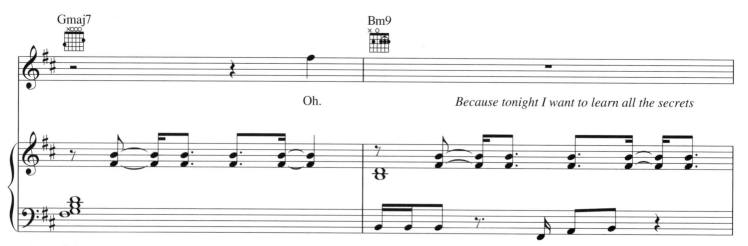

Oh.

Because tonight I want to learn all the secrets

* *Recorded a half step lower.*

in your garden.

I want to read ___ your mind, ___ know your deep -
___ - o - dy ___ we can sing ___
be with you, ___ let me lay ___
___ of you, ___ that's what a

- est feel - ings. I want to make ___ it ___ right for ___ you. ___
___ to - geth - er. I've got the se - cret ___ key to you, ba - by. ___
___ be - side ___ you, do what you want ___ me ___ to all ___ night. ___
man is s'posed to do. And I'll be there ___ for ___ you all the time. ___

THEME FROM SHAFT
from SHAFT

Words and Music by
ISAAC HAYES

Moderately

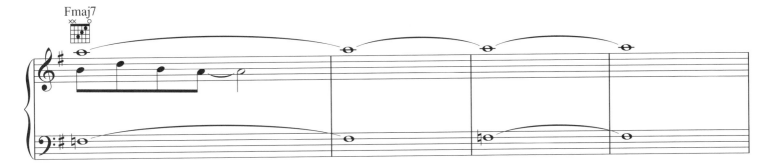

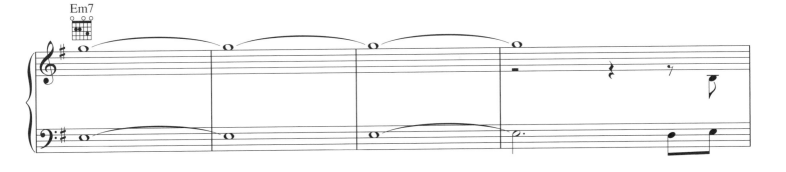

(Spoken:) Who's the black pri-vate dick ___ that's a sex ma-chine to all the chicks?   (Shaft!)

You're damn right!

Who   is the man   that would   risk his life for his broth-er   man? _   (Shaft!)

no one un-der-stands him but his wom-an.   (John   Shaft!)

SEPTEMBER

Words and Music by MAURICE WHITE,
AL McKAY and ALLEE WILLIS

Moderate Rock

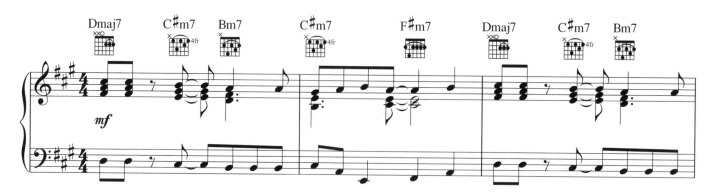

1. Do you re - mem - ber the
2. ring - ing in the key
3., 4. (See additional lyrics)

twen - ty - first night of Sep - tem - ber?   Love was
that our souls were sing - ing   as we

379

Additional Lyrics

3. My thoughts are with you,
   Holding hands with your heart,
   To see you, only blue talk and love.
   Remember how we knew love was here to stay?

4. Now December found the love that we shared,
   September, only blue talk and love.
   Remember the true love we share today.
   Chorus

(Sittin' On)
THE DOCK OF THE BAY

Words and Music by STEVE CROPPER
and OTIS REDDING

SHOT GUN

Words and Music by
AUTRY DeWALT

I said

385

Repeat ad lib. and Fade

SINCE I LOST MY BABY

Words and Music by WILLIAM ROBINSON, JR.
and WARREN MOORE

Moderately slow

Sun is shin - ing,   there's plen - ty of   light. __
Birds are sing - ing,   chil - dren are   play - ing.
De - ter - mi - na - tion   is   fad - ing   fast. __

D.S. al Coda

STOP! IN THE NAME OF LOVE

Words and Music by LAMONT DOZIER,
BRIAN HOLLAND and EDWARD HOLLAND

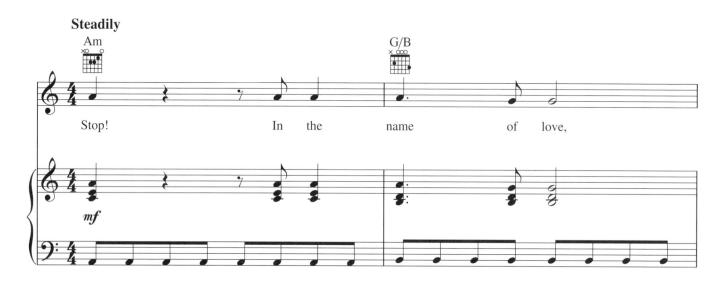

Stop! In the name of love,

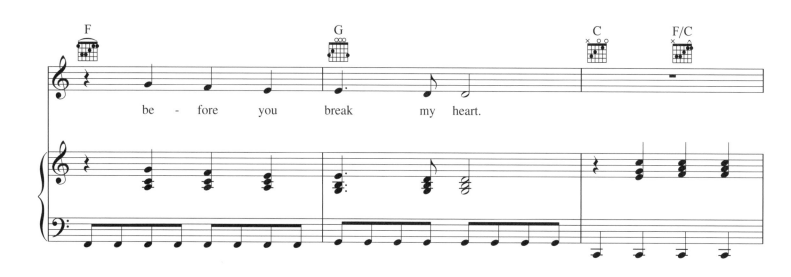

be - fore you break my heart.

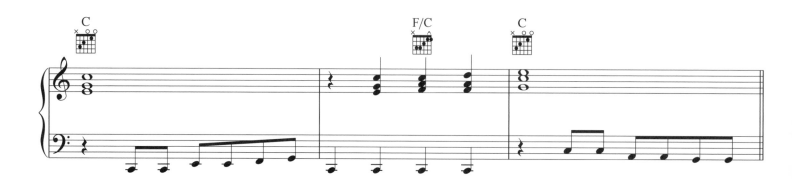

STRAWBERRY LETTER 23

Words and Music by
SHUGGIE OTIS

The mus - ic plays, I sit in for _____ a few. _____

Ooh. _____

Ooh. _____

Ooh. _____

Repeat and Fade | **Optional Ending**

Ooh. _____

SWEET THING
(Sweet Thang)

Words and Music by CHAKA KHAN
and TONY MAIDEN

I would love you an-y-way, even if you can-not stay.
I wish you were my lov-er, but you act so un-der-cov-er.

I think you are the one ___ for me, here is where you ought ___ to be. ___
I love you, child, my whole ___ life long, be it right, or be ___ it wrong. ___

I just__ want to sat - is - fy you, though__ you're not mine, I can't de - ny it.

Don't you hear me talk - ing, ba - by? Love me now or...

You're my heat, you're my fire. You're not mine, can't de - ny __ it.

Repeat ad lib. and Fade | **Optional Ending**

Don't you hear me talk - ing, ba - by? Love me now or I'll go cra - zy.

THE TEARS OF A CLOWN

Words and Music by STEVIE WONDER,
WILLIAM "SMOKEY" ROBINSON and HENRY COSBY

Oh, yeah.

Now, if there's a smile ___ up - on my face, ___ it's on - ly there ___
___ to be care - free, ___ it's on - ly to cam -

D.S. (See additional lyrics)

___ try - ing to fool ___ the pub - lic. But when it comes ___ down to fool - ing you, ___
- ou - flage ___ my sad - ness. In or - der to shield ___ my ___ pride, I try ___

Additional Lyrics

Now, if there's a smile on my face,
Don't let my glad expression
Give you a wrong impression.
Don't let this smile I wear
Make you think that I don't care. *(Fade)*

TAKE ME TO THE RIVER

Words and Music by AL GREEN
and MABON HODGES

(1.,3.) I don't know why   I
(2.) I don't know why   you

love you like I do, ___   af-ter all these chang-es   that you put me through. ___
treat-ed me so bad. ___   Look at all these things ___   that we could have had. ___

THINK

Words and Music by
LOWMAN PAULING

THIS OLD HEART OF MINE
(Is Weak for You)

Words and Music by BRIAN HOLLAND, LAMONT DOZIER,
EDWARD HOLLAND and SYLVIA MOY

Additional Lyrics

2. I try hard to hide my hurt inside.
   This old heart of mine always keeps me cryin'.
   I try hard to hide my hurt inside.
   This old heart of mine always keeps me cryin' the way you treat me,
   Leaves me incomplete, you're here for the day, gone for the week, now.
   But if you leave me a hundred times,
   A hundred times I'll take you back.
   I'm yours whenever you want me,
   I'm not too proud to shout it.
   Tell the world about it 'cause I love you.

THIS WILL BE
(An Everlasting Love)

Words and Music by MARVIN YANCY
and CHUCK JACKSON

TIME WILL REVEAL

Words and Music by BUNNY DeBARGE
and ELDRA DeBARGE

What can I do _____ to make you feel __ se - cure? __
Time will show the val - ue _____ of just what you mean __ to me. __
I tell you I love __ you, ___ but you won't be - lieve __ it's true. __

Instrumental

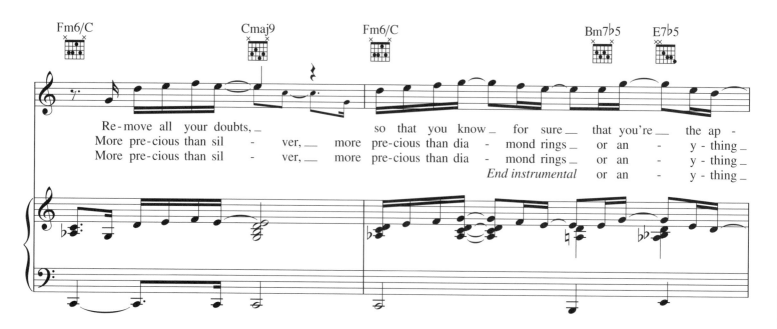

Re - move all your doubts, _ so that you know __ for sure __ that you're __ the ap -
More pre-cious than sil - ver, __ more pre-cious than dia - mond rings __ or an - y - thing __
More pre-cious than sil - ver, __ more pre-cious than dia - mond rings __ or an - y - thing __

End instrumental or an - y - thing __

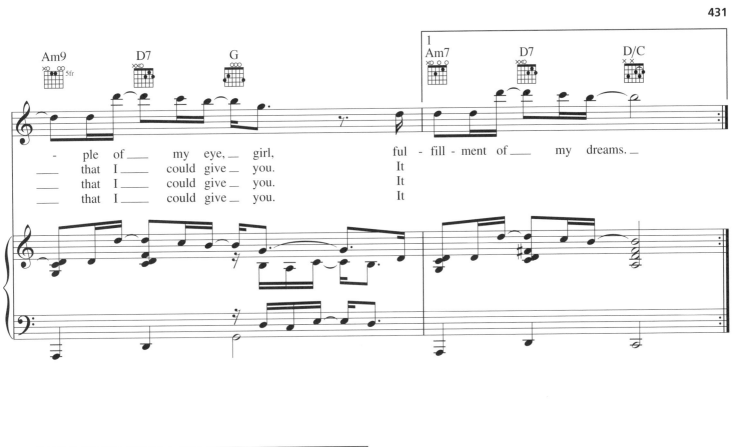

TRAMP

Words and Music by LOWELL FULSOM
and JIMMY McCRACKLIN

(Otis:) Tramp?   (Carla:) That's right, that's what you are.

G7   F7   C   **D.C. al Coda**
(See Additional Lyrics)

Repeat and Fade | **Optional Ending**
(Ad lib. dialogue) | C

CODA   C7

Additional Lyrics

Carla: You know what, Otis, I don't care what you say,
You're still a tramp.

Otis: What?

That's right, you don't even have a fat bankroll
in your pocket. You probably haven't even got
twenty-five cents.

I got six Cadillacs, five Lincolns, four Olds,
six Mercurys, three T-birds, a Mustang...
To Chorus:

UNTIL YOU COME BACK TO ME
(That's What I'm Gonna Do)

Words and Music by STEVIE WONDER,
MORRIS BROADNAX and CLARENCE O. PAUL

WE'VE COME TOO FAR TO END IT NOW

Words and Music by JOHN BRISTOL,
WADE BROWN, JR. and DAVID JONES, JR.

Moderate groove

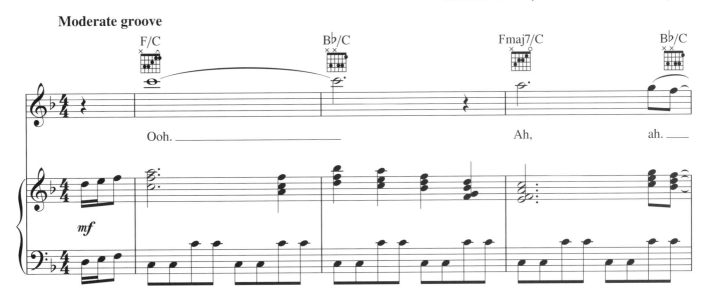

Ooh. _____ Ah, ah. _____

Last

night we had an ar-gu-ment. _____ Oh, _____ oh, _____

Gm7
B♭/C
Fmaj7
be so ver - y wrong.
Oh.
F7
Gm7
We've had ar - gu - ments be -
C7
A
fore but there's one thing you must
Dm
B♭m6/D♭
2fr
F/C
know that we've come too

WHAT YOU WON'T DO FOR LOVE

Words and Music by BOBBY CALDWELL
and ALFONS KETTNER

A WOMAN, A LOVER, A FRIEND

Words and Music by
SID WYCHE

WHAT'D I SAY

Words and Music by
RAY CHARLES

Medium Bounce

WHEN SOMETHING IS WRONG WITH MY BABY

Words and Music by ISAAC HAYES
and DAVID PORTER

When some-thin' is wrong ___ with my

ba - by, ___   some-thin' is

wrong ___ with me.   And if I

* Recorded a half step higher.

YESTER-ME, YESTER-YOU, YESTERDAY

Words by RON MILLER
Music by BRYAN WELLS

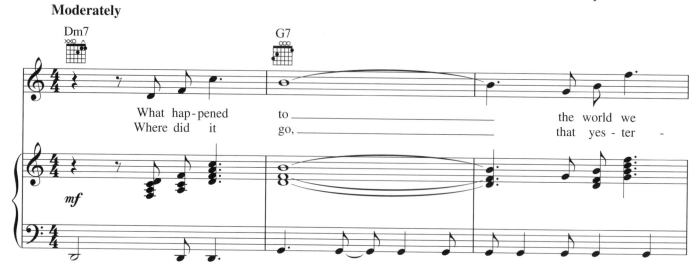

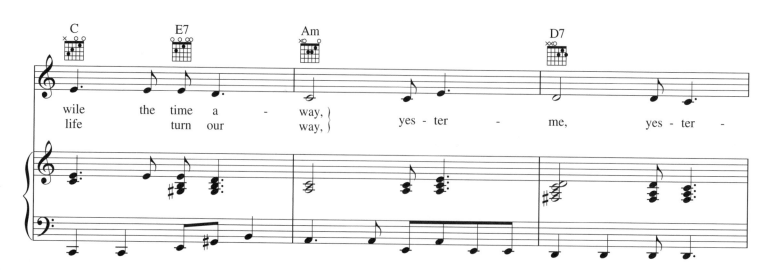

YOU CAN MAKE IT IF YOU TRY

Words and Music by
TED JARRETT

Moderate Funk

You can make it if you try. ___

You can make it ___ if you try. ___

Push   a ___ lit-tle   hard ___ er,   think   a lit-tle   deep ___ er. ___
Time   still ___ creep ___ ing,   'spe-cial-ly   when you're   sleep ___ ing. ___
You'll   get ___ what's   due ___ you,   ev-'ry-thing com-ing   to   you. ___

*Recorded a half step higher.

D.S. al Coda

CODA

D7	G7	C

yeah,   yeah,   yeah.

A7/C♯	D7	C

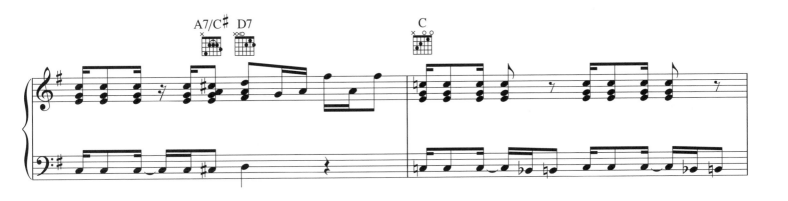

YOU'RE THE FIRST, THE LAST, MY EVERYTHING

Words and Music by P. STERLING RADCLIFFE,
TONY SEPE and BARRY WHITE

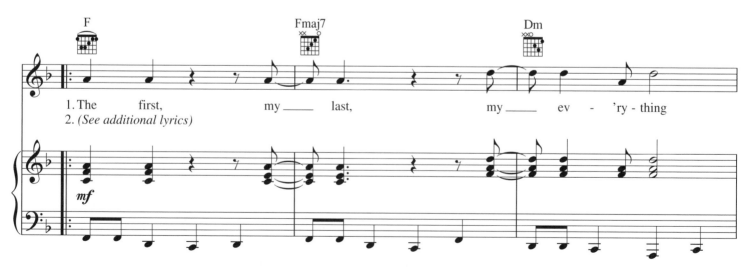

the first,

the last, __ my ev-'ry-thing.

Additional Lyrics

2. In you I find so many things,
   A love so new only you could bring.
   Can't you see if you... you make me feel this way,
   You're like a fresh morning dew
   Or a brand-new day.

   I see so many ways that I
   Can love you till the day I die.
   You're my reality,
   Yet I'm lost in a dream.
   You're the first, the last, my everything.

YOUR PRECIOUS LOVE

Words and Music by NICKOLAS ASHFORD
and VALERIE SIMPSON

Moderately

1. Ev-'ry day __ there's some-thing new, __
2.,3. (See additional lyrics)

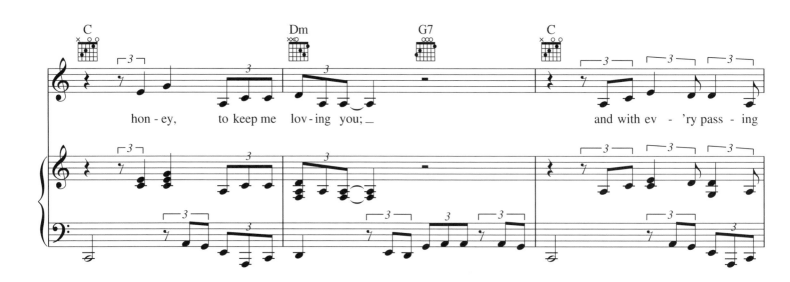

hon-ey, to keep me lov-ing you; __ and with ev-'ry pass-ing

min-ute so much joy ____ wrapped up in it. Oh, ____

CODA

Heav - en must have sent you from a - bove. _____ Oh, _____

heav - en must have sent your _____ pre - cious love. _____

Repeat and Fade

Additional Lyrics

2. And now I've got a song to sing
   Tellin' the world about the joy you bring.
   And you gave me a reason for living
   And, ooh, you taught me the meaning of giving, ooh.

3. *Male:* What you've given me I could never return
   'Cause there's so much girl, I've yet to learn.
   Female: And I want to show my appreciation
   'Cause when I found you I found a new inspiration.
   Both: Oh, heaven must have sent you from above.
   Oh, heaven must have sent your precious love. Oh...
   Coda

ZOOM

Words and Music by LIONEL RICHIE
and RONALD LaPREAD

Whoa, I'd like to greet the sun each morn - ing

and walk a-mongst the stars at night._____ I'd like to know the

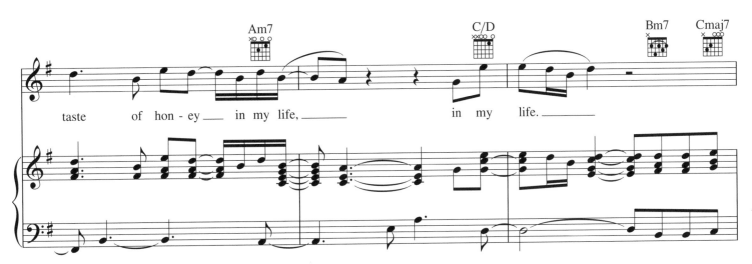

taste of hon - ey ___ in my life, _____ in my life. _____

Recorded a half step lower.

Hal Leonard
ANTHOLOGY SONGBOOKS

These collections set the gold standard for 100 prime songs at an affordable price.

All titles arranged for piano and voice with guitar chords.

ANTHOLOGY OF BROADWAY SONGS – GOLD EDITION

100 beloved songs from the Great White Way, including: All I Ask of You • Day by Day • Good Morning Baltimore • Guys and Dolls • It's De-Lovely • Makin' Whoopee! • My Favorite Things • On the Street Where You Live • Send in the Clowns • They Call the Wind Maria • Written in the Stars • Younger Than Springtime • and more.
00311954 P/V/G $24.99

ANTHOLOGY OF CHRISTMAS SONGS – GOLD EDITION

A cream-of-the-crop collection of 100 holiday favorites, both secular and sacred, including: All I Want for Christmas Is You • Carol of the Bells • Dance of the Sugar Plum Fairy • The First Noel • Jingle-Bell Rock • Joy to the World • O Christmas Tree • Santa Baby • Up on the Housetop • What Child Is This? • and more.
00311998 P/V/G $24.99

ANTHOLOGY OF JAZZ SONGS – GOLD EDITION

This solid collection of jazz favorites boasts 100 songs that set the gold standard for jazz classics! Includes: All of You • April in Paris • Come Fly with Me • From This Moment On • I Got It Bad and That Ain't Good • In the Mood • Lazy River • St. Louis Blues • Stormy Weather (Keeps Rainin' All the Time) • When I Fall in Love • and dozens more.
00311952 P/V/G $24.99

ANTHOLOGY OF LATIN SONGS – GOLD EDITION

100 Latin-flavored favorites, including: Bésame Mucho (Kiss Me Much) • Cast Your Fate to the Wind • Desafinado • La Bamba • Mas Que Nada • One Note Samba (Samba De Uma Nota So) • Quiet Nights of Quiet Stars (Corcovado) • So Nice (Summer Samba) • Spanish Eyes • Sway (Quien Sera) • and more.
00311956 P/V/G $24.99

ANTHOLOGY OF LOVE SONGS – GOLD EDITION

This fantastic collection features 100 songs full of love and romance, including: And I Love You So • Cheek to Cheek • Crazy • Fields of Gold • Grow Old with Me • Just the Way You Are • Love Me Tender • On a Slow Boat to China • Take My Breath Away (Love Theme) • A Time for Us (Love Theme) • Unchained Melody • When I Need You • and more.
00311955 P/V/G $24.99

ANTHOLOGY OF MOVIE SONGS – GOLD EDITION

An outstanding collection of favorite cinema songs, including: Bella's Lullaby • Dancing Queen • Georgia on My Mind • I Will Always Love You • Love Story • Mission: Impossible Theme • Theme from The Simpsons • Take My Breath Away (Love Theme) • A Whole New World • You Are the Music in Me • and many more.
00311967 P/V/G $24.99

ANTHOLOGY OF R&B SONGS – GOLD EDITION

100 R&B classics are included in this collection: ABC • Brick House • Get Ready • I Say a Little Prayer • It's Your Thing • Mustang Sally • Please Mr. Postman • Respect • This Old Heart of Mine (Is Weak for You) • What'd I Say • and more.
00312016 P/V/G $24.99

ANTHOLOGY OF ROCK SONGS – GOLD EDITION

This amazing collection features 100 rock hits, including: Africa • Bad, Bad Leroy Brown • Chantilly Lace • December 1963 (Oh, What a Night) • Fun, Fun, Fun • A Hard Day's Night • Layla • Night Moves • Ramblin' Man • That'll Be the Day • We Will Rock You • and many more.
00311953 P/V/G $24.99